Raptc̲

Written by
Jill Atkins

Rans❀m

Raptors are birds that hunt,
kill and eat meat.

They fly back and forth
across the land, often hunting
at dawn or dusk, looking for food.

There are lots of different kinds of raptors. Here are some of them.

The **buzzard** is a common brown raptor. Buzzards can often be seen flying over woodland.

Their wings are wide and round, with finger-like ends.

Crows sometimes bombard a buzzard in the air if they think it will take their eggs or chicks.

The **red kite**.

In the 1930s, there were very few red kites in the United Kingdom, but now there are many.

Kites have brown, black and white wings and a red fan-shaped tail.

Kites do not often kill animals for food. They feed mainly on dead animals that they find.

Kestrels are small, tan, black and white birds.

They often hover by the side of main roads, looking for food, but they can be found on farmland and in towns, too.

Owls hunt for food at night.

They have large round eyes to see in the dark.

Owls have a flat face and their eyes face forwards.

Their flat face helps them hear the sounds of their prey.

Raptors eat small mammals like mice and shrews, as well as frogs, insects and small birds.

Some bigger raptors eat small rabbits and fish.

Raptors have very sharp eyesight. They can see much better than people.

So they can spot their food from high up in the sky, or in the darkness of night.

Raptors have a wide wing span and they can hover or float on the wind. Their wings make no sound. Their prey suspect nothing!

When the raptor sees something to eat, it dives down. The animal or bird cannot escape.

Raptors have strong sharp claws called talons to grip their food.

The beaks of raptors are like very sharp hooks for ripping the meat.

Sometimes, raptors take birds' eggs or chicks from nests.

Crows' nests are at the tops of trees, so the eggs and chicks are easy to spot.

Crows' nests at the top of a tree.

If a raptor is sick or hurt,
it can go to a bird hospital,
where people will help
make it better.

Some raptors go through
training so people can
meet them and see
them fly and hunt.